Grace W. Davis

Gems of Gospel Songs

.

Grace W. Davis

Gems of Gospel Songs

ISBN/EAN: 9783337181710

Printed in Europe, USA, Canada, Australia, Japan

Cover: Foto ©Lupo / pixelio.de

More available books at **www.hansebooks.com**

GEMS

OF

GOSPEL SONGS

GATHERED BY

Grace Weiser Davis.

Published for the author by
JOHN J. HOOD,
1018 Arch St., Phila., Pa.

INDEX.

GEMS OF

GOSPEL SONGS.

Music No. 261 in " The Temple Trio."

'TIS a story oft repeated, but it never can grow old,
The story of the blood that makes us clean;
'tis the sweetest story ears have heard or lips have
The blood of Jesus cleanseth from all sin. [ever told,

Cho.—Able to save to the uttermost,
He offers us cleansing, and oh, it is free!
Wondrous salvation! it saves even me!
Washed in the blood of the Lamb.

Now it rings through earth and heaven, sung by ran-
somed choirs above,
Who by its power o'ercame and were made clean;
Now 'tis echoed by the pure of earth, saved by re-
deeming love;
The blood of Jesus cleanseth from all sin.

As I listen to the message, how it thrills me with de-
The fountain now is open—enter in;   [light;
Whosoever will may venture in and wash his gar-
ments white;
The blood of Jesus cleanseth from all sin.

Then why should I tarry longer? Jesus' call I will
I come, I wash, the promised rest I win,   [obey;
will trust his power to keep me clean each moment,
every day;
The blood of Jesus cleanseth from all sin.

O this wonderful salvation—praise the dear Redeem-
It reaches me,—his praise I must begin; [er's name!
'tis my greatest joy, with all the saved forever to .
proclaim,
The blood of Jesus cleanseth from all sin.

3

HOVER o'er me, Holy Spirit;
   Bathe my trembling heart and brow;
Fill me with thy hallowed presence,—
   Come, oh, come and fill me now.

CHO.—Fill me now, fill me now,
   Jesus, come and fill me now;
   Fill me with thy hallowed presence,—
   Come, oh, come and fill me now.

2 Thou canst fill me, gracious Spirit,
   Though I cannot tell thee how;
But I need thee, greatly need thee;
   Come, oh, come and fill me now.

3 I am weakness, full of weakness;
   At thy sacred feet I bow;
Blest, divine, eternal Spirit,
   Fill with power, and fill me now.

4 Cleanse and comfort, bless and save me;
   Bathe, oh, bathe my heart and brow;
Thou art comforting and saving,
   Thou art sweetly filling now.

3   *Temple Songs, No. 179.*

MY soul, in sad exile, was out on life's sea,
   So burdened with sin, and distrest. [choice;
Till I heard a sweet voice, saying, make me your
   And I entered the "Haven of Rest!"

CHO.—I've anchored my soul in the haven of rest,
   I'll sail the wide seas no more;   [deep,
   The tempest may sweep o'er the wild, stormy
   In Jesus I'm safe evermore.

2 I yielded myself to his tender embrace,
   And faith taking hold of the word,
My fetters fell off, and I anchored my soul;
   The haven of rest is my Lord.

3 The song of my soul, since the Lord made me whole,
   Has been the OLD STORY so blest
Of Jesus, who'll save whosoever will have
   A home in the "Haven of Rest."

4 How precious the thought that we all may recline,
   Like John the beloved and blest,
On Jesus' strong arm, where no tempest can harm,—
   Secure in the "Haven of rest."

5 Oh, come to the Saviour, he patiently waits
   To save by his power divine;
Come, anchor your soul in the haven of rest,
   And say, "my Beloved is mine."

4   *Music No. 30 in " The Quartet."*

THOUGH troubles assail, and dangers affright,
   Though friends should all fail, and foes all unite,
Yet one thing secures us, whatever betide,
The promise assures us,—the Lord will provide.

CHO.—Yes, I will rejoice, rejoice in the Lord,
    Yes, I will rejoice, rejoice in the Lord,
    Yes, I will rejoice, rejoice in the Lord,
     Will joy in the God of my salvation.

2 The birds, without barn or storehouse, are fed;
From them let us learn to trust for our bread,
His saints, what is fitting, shall ne'er be denied,
So long as 'tis written,—the Lord will provide.

3 When Satan appears to stop up our path,
And fills us with fears, we triumph by faith;
He cannot take from us, though oft he has tried,
The heart-cheering promise,—the Lord will provide.

4 He tells us we're weak,—our hope is in vain:
The good that we seek we ne'er shall obtain:
But when such suggestions our graces have tried,
This answers all questions,—the Lord will provide.

5 No strength of our own, nor goodness we claim;
Our trust is all thrown on Jesus' great name:
In this our strong tower for safety we hide;
The Lord is our power,—the Lord will provide.

6 When life sinks apace, and death is in view,
The word of his grace shall comfort us through:
Not fearing or doubting, with Christ on our side,
We hope to die shouting,—the Lord will provide.

I AM dwelling on the mountain,
　Where the golden sunlight gleams
O'er a land whose wondrous beauty
　Far exceeds my fondest dreams.
Where the air is pure ethereal,
　Laden with the breath of flowers,
They are blooming by the fountain,
　'Neath the amaranthine bowers.

CHO.—Is not this the land of Beulah,
　　Blessed, blessed land of light,
　　Where the flowers bloom forever,
　　And the sun is always bright?

2 I can see far down the mountain,
　Where I wandered weary years,
Often hindered in my journey
　By the ghosts of doubts and fears,
Broken vows and disappointments
　Thickly sprinkled all the way,
But the Spirit led, unerring,
　To the land I hold to-day.

3 I am drinking at the fountain,
　Where I ever would abide;
For I've tasted life's pure river,
　And my soul is satisfied;
There's no thirsting for life's pleasures,
　Nor adorning, rich and gay,
For I've found a richer treasure,
　One that fadeth not away.

5 Oh, the Cross has wondrous glory.
　Oft I've proved this to be true;
When I'm in the way so narrow
　I can see a pathway through;
And how sweetly Jesus whispers:
　Take the Cross, thou need'st not fear,
For I've tried this way before thee,
　And the glory lingers near.

6

COME to Jesus, come to Jesus,
   Come to Jesus just now,
Just now come to Jesus,
   Come to Jesus just now.

2 He will save you.
3 Oh, believe him.
4 He is able.
5 He is willing.
6 He'll receive you.
7 Flee to Jesus.
8 Call unto him.

9 He will hear you.
10 He'll have mercy.
11 He'll forgive you.
12 He will cleanse you.
13 He'll renew you.
14 He will clothe you.
15 Jesus loves you.

7

REDEEMED, how I love to proclaim it,
   Redeemed by the blood of the Lamb;
Redeemed through his infinite mercy,
   His child and forever I am.

CHO.—   Redeemed, redeemed,
   Redeemed by the blood of the Lamb;
   Redeemed, redeemed,
   His child and forever I am.

2 Redeemed, and so happy in Jesus,
   No language my rapture can tell,
I know that the light of his presence
   With me doth continually dwell.

3 I think of my blessed Redeemer,
   I think of him all the day long,
I sing, for I cannot be silent,
   His love is the theme of my song.

4 I know I shall see in his beauty
   The King in whose law I delight,
Who lovingly guardeth my footsteps,
   And giveth me songs in the night.

5 I know there's a crown that is waiting
   In yonder bright mansion for me,
And soon, with the spirits made perfect,
   At home with the Lord I shall be.

8

Music No. 288 in " The Temple Trio."

MY life, my love I give to thee,
    Thou Lamb of God, who died for me;
Oh, may I ever faithful be,
    My Saviour and my God!

CHO.—I'll live for him who died for me,
    How happy then my life shall be!
    I'll live for him who died for me,
    My Saviour and my God!

2 I now believe thou dost receive,
    For thou hast died that I might live;
    And now henceforth I'll trust in thee,
    My Saviour and my God!

3 Oh, thou who died on Calvary,
    To save my soul and make me free,
    I consecrate my life to thee,
    My Saviour and my God!

9   *Music No. 324 in " The Temple Trio."*

THERE are songs of joy that I loved to sing
    When my heart was as blithe as a bird in spring;
But the song I have learned is so full of cheer,
That the dawn shines out in the darkness drear.

CHO.—O the new, new song! O the new, new song!
    I can sing it now with the ransomed throng:
    Power and dominion to him that shall reign:
    Glory and praise to the Lamb that was slain!

2 There are strains of home that are dear as life,
And I list to them oft 'mid the din of strife;
But I know of a home that is wondrous fair,
And I sing the psalm they are singing there.

3 Can my lips be mute, or my heart be sad,
When the gracious Master hath made me glad?
When he points where the many mansions be,
And sweetly says, "There is one for thee"?

4 I shall catch the gleam of its jasper wall
When I come to the gloom of the evenfall;
For I know that the shadows, dreary and dim,
Have a path of light that will lead to him.

8

THERE'S a crown in heaven for the striving soul,
  Which the blessed Jesus himself will place
On the head of each who shall faithful prove,
  Even unto death, in the heavenly race.
REF.—Oh, may that crown in heaven be mine,
  And I among the angels shine:
  Be thou, O Lord, my daily guide,
  Let me ever in thy love abide.

2 There's a joy in heaven for the mourning soul,
  Though the tears may fall all the earthly night;
Yet the clouds of sadness will break away,
  And rejoicing come with the morning light.
REF.—Oh, may that joy in heaven, etc.

3 There's a home in heaven for the faithful soul,
  In the many mansions prepared above,
Where the glorified shall forever sing,
  Of a Saviour's free and unbounded love.
REF.—Oh, may that home in heaven, etc.

COME, thou Fount of every blessing,
  Tune my heart to sing thy grace;
Streams of mercy, never ceasing,
  Call for songs of loudest praise.
CHO.—Oh, 'tis glory! oh, 'tis glory!
  Oh, 'tis glory in my soul,
  For I've touched the hem of his garment,
  And his power doth make me whole.

2 Teach me some melodious sonnet,
  Sung by flaming tongues above;
Praise the mount—I'm fixed upon it—
  Mount of thy redeeming love!

3 Here I'll raise mine Ebenezer;
  Hither by thy help I'm come;
And I hope, by thy good pleasure,
  Safely to arrive at home.

4 Jesus sought me when a stranger,
  Wandering from the fold of God;
He, to rescue me from danger,
  Interposed his precious blood.

12

WE shall walk the realms of glory,
  Where eternal beauty reigns.
There, with seraph hosts unnumbered,
  Join the grand immortal strains.

CHO.—We shall walk the realms of glory,
    With the loved ones gone before,
  We shall sing the sweet old story,
    Over on the other shore.

2 We shall walk the realms of glory
    With the bloodwashed, mighty throng,
  We shall join the angel harpers
    In their everlasting song.

3 We shall walk the realms of glory,
    And by Jesus' side sit down;
  Clad no more in robes of sorrow,
    We shall wear a fadeless crown.

4 We shall walk the realms of glory,
    Where no tears can ever come,
  Where the sunlight is not needed,
    In that sweet, eternal home.

13

LORD, I care not for riches,
  Neither silver nor gold;
I would make sure of heaven,
  I would enter the fold;
In the book of thy kingdom,
  With its pages so fair,
Tell me, Jesus, my Saviour,
  Is my name written there?

CHO.—Is my name written there,
    On the page white and fair?
  In the book of thy kingdom,
    Is my name written there?

2 Lord, my sins they are many,
  Like the sands of the sea;
But thy blood, O my Saviour,
  Is sufficient for me;

10

For thy promise is written
In bright letters that glow,
"Though your sins be as scarlet,
I will make them like snow."

3 Oh! that beautiful city,
With its mansions of light,
With its glorified beings,
In pure garments of white;
Where no evil thing cometh,
To despoil what is fair;
Where the angels are watching,—
Is my name written there?

14 *Music No. 25 in " The Quartet."*

THERE is a fountain ||: filled with blood, :||
Drawn from Immanuel's veins,
And sinners plunged ||: beneath that flood, :||
Lose all their guilty stains.

Cho.—Oh, glorious fountain!
Here will I stay,
And in thee ever
Wash my sins away.

2 The dying thief ||: rejoiced to see :||
That fountain in his day,
And there may I, ||: though vile as he, :||
Wash all my sins away,

3 Thou dying Lamb, ||: thy precious blood :||
Shall never lose its power,
Till all the ransomed ||: Church of. God :||
Are saved, to sin no more.

4 E'er since by faith ||: I saw the stream :||
Thy flowing wounds supply,
Redeeming love ||: has been my theme, :||
And shall be till I die.

5 When this poor lisping, ||: stamm'ring tongue :||
Lies silent in the grave,
Then in a nobler, ||: sweeter song, :||
I'll sing thy power to save.

OH, where are the reapers that garner in
The sheaves of the good from the fields of sin;
With sickles of truth must the work be done,
And no one may rest till the "harvest home."

CHO.—Where are the reapers! oh, who will come
And share in the glory of the "harvest h me?"
Oh, who will help us to garner in
The sheaves of good from the fields of sin?

2 Go out in the byways and search them all;
The wheat may be there, though the weeds are tall;
Then search in the highway, and pass none by,
But gather from all for the home on high.

3 The fields all are ripening, and far and wide
The world now is waiting the harvest-tide:
But the reapers are few, and the work is great,
And much will be lost should the harvest wait.

4 So come with your sickles, ye sons of men,
And gather together the golden grain;
Toil on till the Lord of the harvest come,
Then share ye his joy in the "harvest home."

OH, how happy are they
Who the Saviour obey,
And have laid up their treasures above;
Tongue can never express
The sweet comfort and peace
Of a soul in its earliest love.

CHO.—Jesus saves me from sin
And his peace dwells within,
And his uttermost salvation I know;
As I walk in the light
Perfect love casts out fear,
And his blood washes whiter than snow.

2 That sweet comfort was mine,
   When the favor divine
I received thro' the blood of the Lamb;
   When my heart first believed,
   What a joy I received—
What a heaven in Jesus' name!

3 'Twas a heaven below
   My Redeemer to know,
And the angels could do nothing **more**
   Than to fall at his feet,
   And the story repeat,
And the Lover of sinners adore.

4 Jesus, all the day long,
   Was my joy and my song;
Oh, that all his salvation might see:
   He hath loved me, I cried,
   He hath suffered and died,
To redeem even rebels like me.

17

O, I LEFT it all with Jesus long ago, long ago, ·
  My sinfulness I brought him and my woe,
And when by faith I saw him on the tree,
And heard his still, small whisper, " 'Tis for thee,"
From my weary heart the burden rolled away, rolled
And now I'm singing glory, happy day.   [away.

2 O, I leave it all with Jesus for he knows, for he knows
Just how to take the bitter from life's woes,
And how to gild the tear-drop with his smile,
To make the desert garden bloom awhile.
Then, with all my weakness leaning on his might, on
My soul sings hallelujah, all is light.   [his might,

3 O, I leave it all with Jesus day by day, day by day,
My faith can firmly trust him, come what may,
For hope has dropped her anchor, found her rest,
Within the calm sure haven of his breast,
And oh! 'tis joy of heaven to abide, to abide
Close to my dear Redeemer, at his side.

13

18

COME, ye sinners, poor and needy,
　　Weak and wounded, sick and **sore;**
Jesus ready stands to save you,
　　Full of pity, love, and power:
　　　　He is able,
　　He is willing: doubt no more.

2 Now, ye needy, come and welcome;
　　God's free bounty glorify;
True belief and true repentance,
　　Every grace that brings you nigh,
　　　　Without money,
　　Come to Jesus Christ and buy.

3 Let not conscience make you linger,
　　Nor of fitness fondly dream;
All the fitness he requireth
　　Is to feel your need of him:
　　　　This he gives you;
　　'Tis the Spirit's glimmering beam.

4 Come, ye weary, heavy-laden,
　　Bruised and mangled by the fall;
If you tarry till you're better,
　　You will never come at all;
　　　　Not the righteous,—
　　Sinners Jesus came to call.

Cho.—Whosoever, whosoever,
　　Whosoever will may come,
Whosoever, saith the Spirit,
　　With the Father and the Son;
Whosoever, sinner, hear it,
　　Whosoever will may come.

19　　*Music No. 78 in "The Quartet."*

SOWING in the morning, sowing seeds of kindness,
　　Sowing in the noon-tide, and the dewy eves;
Waiting for the harvest, and the time of reaping,
　We shall come rejoicing, bringing in the sheaves.

Cho.—Bringing in the sheaves, bringing in the sheaves,
　　We shall come rejoicing, bringing in the sheaves.:‖

2 Sowing in the sunshine, sowing in the shadows,
　Fearing neither clouds nor winter's chill ng breeze;
By and by the harvest, and the labor ended,
　We shall come rejoicing, bringing in the sheaves.

3 Go, then, ever weeping, sowing for the Master,
　Though the loss sustained our spirit often grieves ;
When our weeping's over, he will bid us welcome,
　We shall come rejoicing, bringing in the sheaves.

20　　　　　*Temple Songs, No. 15.*

FRIENDS of yore have flown to heaven,
　　Springing from the house of clay ;
Glad to gain their joyful freedom,
　Borne by angel bands away.

Cho.—While on Pisgah's mount I'm standing,
　　Looking t'ward the vernal shore,
　There I seem to see them banding,
　Just beside the Golden Landing,
　　Waiting to receive me o'er,
　Precious ones who ve gone before!

2 Often at the shades of evening,
　　When I sit me down to rest,
　One by one I count them over,
　　They who are in glory blest.

3 And I seem to see their faces,
　　Beaming with celestial love,
　Shining as their blessed Master,
　　White robed, with the saints above.

4 And I think I hear them speaking,
　　As they often spake to me,
　While I seem to hear them saying,
　　"Pilgrim, heaven is waiting thee."

5 Brother, sister, faithful soldier,
　　If our mingling here so sweet,
　What shall be our joyous rapture
　　When we at the landing meet !

21

I HAVE found repose for my weary soul,
    Trusting in the promise of the Saviour;
And a harbor safe when the billows roll,
    Trusting in the promise of the Saviour.
I will fear no foe in the deadly strife,
    Trusting in the promise of the Saviour;
I will bear my lot in the toil of life,
    Trusting in the promise of the Saviour.

REF.—Resting on his mighty arm forever,
    Never from his loving heart to sever,
    I will rest by grace in his strong embrace,
    Trusting in the promise of the Saviour.

2 I will sing my song as the days go by,
    Trusting in the promise of the Saviour;
And rejoice in hope, while I live or die,
    Trusting in the promise of the Saviour.
I can smile at grief, and abide in pain,
    Trusting in the promise of the Saviour;
And the loss of all shall be highest gain,
    Trusting in the promise of the Saviour.

3 Oh, the peace and joy of the life I live,
    Trusting in the promise of the Saviour;
Oh, the strength and love only God can give,
    Trusting in the promise of the Saviour.
Whosoever will may be saved to-day,
    Trusting in the promise of the Saviour;
And begin to walk in the holy way,
    Trusting in the promise of the Saviour.

22

O JESUS, Lord, thy dying love
    Hath pierced my contrite heart;
Now take my life, and let me prove
    How dear to me thou art.

CHO.—At the cross, ‖ where I first saw the light,
    And the burden of my heart rolled away,
    It was there by faith I received my sight,
    And now I am happy night and day!

2 Amid the night of sin and death
   Thy light hath filled my soul;
To me thy loving voice now saith,
   Thy faith hath made thee whole,

3 I kiss thy feet, I clasp thy hand,
   I touch thy bleeding side;
O let me here forever stand,
   Where thou wast crucified.

4 My Lord, my light, my strength, my all,
   I count my gain but loss;
Forever let thy love enthrall,
   And keep me at the cross.   —R. K. CARTER.

23 *Copyright, 1885, by J. J. Hood.   Tune,"Close to Thee."*

SAVIOUR of the weak and weary,
   My unworthiness I see;
But thy loveliness hath charmed me,
And I want to walk with thee.
||: Close to thee, close to thee; :||
   But thy loveliness, etc.

2 Lead me to the cleansing fountain,
   From defilement set me free;
Put thine image, Lord, upon me,
That I may walk close to thee.
||: Close to thee, close to thee; :||
   Put thine image, etc.

3 If at times the way seems lonely,
   If thy face I cannot see,
Whisper some sweet words of promise;
Tell me I am close to thee.
||: Close to thee, close to thee; :||
   Whisper some, etc.

4 May each hour—and every moment—
   Glad with thine own image be,
Till thy voice shall call me homeward,
Evermore to dwell with thee.
||: Close to thee, close to thee; :||
   Till thy voice, etc.

JESUS, thine all-victorious love
    Shed in my heart abroad:
Then shall my feet no longer rove,
    Rooted and fixed in God.

2 O that in me the sacred fire
    Might now begin to glow,
Burn up the dross of base desire
    And make me mountains flow!

3 O that it now from heaven might fall,
    And all my sins consume!
Come, Holy Ghost, for thee I call;
    Spirit of burning, come!

4 Refining fire, go thro' my heart;
    Illuminate my soul;
Scatter thy life thro' every part,
    And sanctify the whole.

5 My steadfast soul, from falling free,
    Shall then no longer move,
While Christ is all the world to me,
    And all my heart is love.   ISAAC WATTS.

25

WE have heard a joyful sound,
    Jesus saves, Jesus saves;
Spread the gladness all around,
·   Jesus saves, Jesus saves;
Bear the news to every land,
    Climb the steeps and cross the waves,
Onward, 'tis our Lord's command,
    Jesus saves, Jesus saves.

2 Waft it on the rolling tide,
    Jesus saves, Jesus saves,
Tell to sinners, far and wide,
    Jesus saves, Jesus saves;
Sing, ye islands of the sea,
    Echo back, ye ocean caves,
Earth shall keep her jubilee,
    Jesus saves, Jesus saves.

3 Sing above the battle's strife,
  Jesus saves, Jesus saves;
By his death and endless life,
  Jesus saves, Jesus saves;
Sing it softly through the gloom,
  When the heart for mercy craves,
Sing in triumph o'er the tomb,
  Jesus saves, Jesus saves.

4 Give the winds a mighty voice,
  Jesus saves, Jesus saves,
Let the nations now rejoice,
  Jesus saves, Jesus saves;
Shout salvation full and free,
  Highest hill and deepest caves,
This our song of victory,
  Jesus saves, Jesus saves.

26   *Music No. 125 in " The Quartet."*

OH, now I see the cleansing wave!
  The fountain deep and wide;
Jesus, my Lord, mighty to save,
  Points to his wounded side.

CHO.—The cleansing stream I see, I see!
    I plunge, and oh, it cleanseth me!
    Oh, praise the Lord! it cleanseth me!
    It cleanseth me, yes, cleanseth me.

2 I see the new creation rise,
  I hear the speaking blood;
It speaks! polluted nature dies!
  Sinks 'neath the cleansing flood.

3 I rise to walk in heaven's own light,
  Above the world of sin,
With heart made pure and garments white,
  And Christ enthroned within.

4 Amazing grace! 'tis heaven below
  To feel the blood applied;
And Jesus, only Jesus, know,
  My Jesus crucified.

27

W ILL you come, will you come, with your poor
    Burdened and sin-oppressed? [broken heart,
Lay it down at the feet of your Saviour and Lord,
    Jesus will give you rest.

REF.—Oh, happy rest! sweet, happy rest!
    Jesus will give you rest,
Oh, why wont you come in simple, trusting faith?
    Jesus will give you rest.

2 Will you come, will you come? there is mercy for you,
    Balm for your aching breast;
Only come as you are, and believe on his name,
    Jesus will give you rest.

3 Will you come, will you come, you have nothing to pay;
    Jesus, who loves you best,
By his death on the cross purchased life for your soul,
    Jesus, will give you rest.

4 Will you come, will you come? how he pleads with
    Fly to his loving breast,   [you now!
And whatever your sin or your sorrow may be,
    Jesus will give you rest.

28

I HOPE to meet you all in glory,
    When the storms of life are o'er;
I hope to tell the dear old story,
    On the blessed shining shore.

CHO.—On the shining shore, on the golden strand
    In our Father's home, in the happy land:
    ‖: I hope to meet you there,— :‖
    A crown of vict'ry wear,—in glory.

2 I hope to meet you all in glory,
    By the tree of life so fair;
I hope to praise our dear Redeemer
    For the grace that brought me there.

3 I hope to meet you all in glory.
    Round the Saviour's throne above;
I hope to join the ransomed army
    Singing now redeeming love.

4 I hope to meet you all in glo y,
When my work on earth is o'er ;
I hope to clasp your hands rejoic ng
On the bright, eternal shore.

29

O N Jordan's stormy banks I stand,
And cast a wishful eye
To Canaan's fair and happy land,
Where my possessions lie.

Cho.—I'll be there, I'll be there,
When the first trumpet sounds I'll be there.

2 O'er all these wide extended plains
Shines one eternal day ;
There God the Son forever reigns,
And scatters night away.

3 When shall I reach that happy place,
And be forever blest ?
When shall I see my Father's face,
And in his bosom rest ?

4 Filled with delight, my raptured soul
Would here no longer stay ;
Though Jordan's waves around me roll,
Fearless I'd launch away.

30
Music No. 151 in " The Quartet."

M Y hope is built on nothing less
Than Jesus' blood and righteousness;
I dare not trust the sweetest frame,
But wholly lean on Jesus' name :

Cho.—On Christ, the Solid Rock, I stand;
||: All other ground is sinking sand. :||

2 When darkness seems to veil his face,
I rest on his unchanging grace;
In every high and stormy gale,
My anchor holds within the vale.

3 His oath, his covenant, and blood,
Support me in the whelming flood :
When all around my soul gives way,
He then is all my hope and stay.

JUST as I am, without one plea,
But that thy blood was shed for me,
And that thou bidst me come to thee,
O Lamb of God, I come!

CHO.—Take me as I am,
Take me as I am;
Oh, bring thy free salvation nigh,
And take me as I am!

2 Just as I am, and waiting not
To rid my soul of one dark blot,
To thee, whose blood can cleanse each spot,
O Lamb of God, I come!

3 Just as I am, though tossed about
With many a conflict, many a doubt,
Fightings within, and fears without,
O Lamb of God, I come!

4 Just as I am—poor, wretched, blind;
Sight, riches, healing of the mind,
Yea, all I need, in thee to find,
O Lamb of God, I come!

5 Just as I am—thou wilt receive,
Wilt welcome, pardon, cleanse, relieve,
Because thy promise I believe,
O Lamb of God, I come!

6 Just as I am—thy love unknown
Hath broken every barrier down;
Now to be thine, yea, thine alone,
O Lamb of God, I come!

32   *Music No. 99 in " The Quartet." New words.*

YE seeking souls, fresh courage take,
For joy cometh in the morning;
A bruised reed will He not break,
For joy cometh in the morning.

CHO.—Joy cometh in the morning;:‖
Weeping may endure, may endure for a night,
But joy cometh in the morning.

2 Ye weeping mourners, dry your tears,
　　For joy cometh in the morning;
　Give to the winds your needless fears,
　　For joy cometh in the morning.

3 Forsake your sins, his word believe,
　　For joy cometh in the morning,
　And you his pardon will receive,
　　For joy cometh in the morning.

4 Our God will wipe away all tears,
　　For joy cometh in the morning;
　Our God will banish all our fears,
　　For joy cometh in the morning.

5 He comes, he comes who frees from sin,
　　For joy cometh in the morning;
　The Joy Giver now enters in,
　　And joy has come with the morning.

33

A ND can I yet delay
　　My little all to give?
To tear myself from earth away
　For Jesus to receive?

Cho.—　I'll never turn back any more,
　　I'll never turn back any more;
There's a mansion for me on the other side of Jordan,
　　And I'll never turn back any more.

2 Nay but I yield, I yield;
　　I can hold out no more:
　I sink, by dying love compelled,
　　And own Thee conqueror.

3 Though late, I all forsake;
　　My friends, my all, resign:
　Gracious Redeemer, take, oh, take
　　And seal me ever thine.

4 Come, and possess me whole,
　　Nor hence again remove;
　Settle and fix my wavering soul
　　With all thy weight of love.

34

Music No. 359 in "The Temple Trio."

ARISE, my soul, arise;
  Shake off thy guilty fears;
The bleeding Sacrifice
  In my behalf appears;
Before the throne my Surety stands,
My name is written on his hands.

2 He ever lives above,
    For me to intercede;
His all-redeeming love,
    His precious blood to plead;
His blood atoned for all our race,
And sprinkles now the throne of grace.

3 Five bleeding wounds he bears,
    Received on Calvary;
They pour effectual prayers,
    They strongly plead for me:
" Forgive him, O forgive," they cry,
" Nor let that ransomed sinner die."

4 The Father hears him pray,
    His dear anointed One:
He cannot turn away
    The presence of his Son:
His Spirit answers to the blood,
And tells me I am born of God.

5 My God is reconciled;
    His pard'ning voice I hear:
He owns me for his child;
    I can no longer fear:
With confidence I now draw,
And, " Father, Abba Father," cry.

35   *Music No. 205 in "The Quartet."*

HAVE you been to Jesus for the cleansing power?
  Are you washed in the blood of the Lamb?
Are you fully trusting in his grace this hour?
  Are you washed in the blood of the Lamb?

CHO.—Are you washed in the blood,
  In the soul-cleansing blood of the Lamb?
Are your garments spotless? are they white as snow!
  Are you washed in the blood of the Lamb?

2 Are you walking daily by the Saviour's side?
Are you washed in the blood of the Lamb?
Do you rest each moment in the Crucified?
Are you washed in the blood of the Lamb?

3 When the Bridegroom cometh, will your robes be
Pure and white in the blood of the Lamb? [white,
Will your soul be ready for the mansions bright,
And be washed in the blood of the Lamb?

4 Lay aside the garments that are stained with sin,
And be washed in the blood of the Lamb;
There's a fountain flowing for the soul unclean,
O be washed in the blood of the Lamb!

36 *Music No. 225 in "The Quartet."*

BEHOLD a stranger at the door,
He gently knocks—has knocked before;
Has waited long, is waiting still;
You treat no other friend so ill.

Cho.—O let the dear Saviour come in,
He'll cleanse the heart from sin;
O keep him no more out at the door,
But let the dear Saviour come in.

2 O lovely attitude,—he stands
With melting heart and open hands;
O matchless kindness, and he shows
This matchless kindness to his foes!

3 But will he prove a friend indeed?
He will,—the very friend you need;
The friend of sinners? Yes, 'tis he,
With garments dyed on Calvary.

4 Rise, touched with gratitude divine;
Turn out his enemy and thine;
That soul-destroying monster, Sin,
And let the heavenly stranger in.

5 Admit him ere his anger burn,—
His feet, departed, ne'er return;
Admit him, or the hour's at hand,
You'll at his door rejected stand.

WHEN you come to Jordan's wave,
    How will you do, how will you do?
You who now contend with God,
    How will you do, how will you do?
Death will be a solemn day;
When the soul is forced away,
It will be too late to pray,—
    How will you do, how will you do?

2 You who have no more than form,
    How will you do, how will you do?
Can you brave that awful storm?
    How will you do, how will you do?
When the hand of death assails,
Every reed and prop must fail,
Forms will be of no avail,—
    How will you do, how will you do?

3 You who have been turned aside,
    How will you do, how will you do?
Whither will you flee to hide?
    How will you do, how will you do?
Can you then the terror brave?
Say you have no soul to save?
When you sink beneath the wave,
    How will you do, how will you do?

4 You who laugh, and scorn, and sneer,
    How will you do, how will you do?
When in judgment you appear,
    How will you do, how will you do?
Conscience will in terror rise,
And the worm that never dies;
When you sink no more to rise,
    How will you do, how will you do?

5 Christian, now I turn to thee,
    How wilt thou do, how wilt thou do?
When thou dost the river see,
    How wilt thou do, how wilt thou do?
To the cross, I then will cling.
Shout, "O death, where is thy sting?"
Victory! victory! I will sing,—
    Thus will I do, thus will I do.

38

WHEN Jesus laid his crown aside,
  He came to save me;
When on the cross he bled and died,
  He came to save me.

Cho.—I'm so glad :‖ that Jesus came,
  And grace is free,
‖: I'm so glad :‖ that Jesus came,
  He came to save me.

2 In my poor heart he deigns to dwell,
  He came to save me;
O, praise his name, I know it well,
  He came to save me.

3 With gentle hand he leads me still,
  He came to save me;
And trusting him I fear no ill,
  He came to save me.

4 To him my faith with rapture clings,
  He came to save me;
To him my heart looks up and sings,
  He came to save me.

39

I AM coming to the cross;
  I am poor, and weak, and blind;
I am counting all but dross,
  I shall full salvation find.

Cho.—I am trusting, Lord, in thee,
  Dear Lamb of Calvary;
Humbly at thy cross I bow,
  Jesus saves, he saves me now.

2 Here, I give my all to thee,
  Friends, and time, and earthly store;
Soul and body thine to be,—
  Wholly thine for evermore.

3 In the promises I trust,
  Now I know the blood applied;
I am prostrate in the dust;
  I with Christ am crucified.

40

DEAR Jesus, I long to be perfectly whole;
I want thee for ever to live in my soul;
Break down every idol, cast out every foe;
Now wash me, and I shall be whiter than snow.

CHO.—Whiter than snow, yes, whiter than snow;
Now wash me, and I shall be whiter than snow.

2 Dear Jesus, let nothing unholy remain;
Apply thine own blood, and extract every stain;
To have this blest washing I all things forego,
Now wash me, and I shall be whiter than snow.

3 Dear Jesus, for this I most humbly entreat;
I wait, blessed Lord, at thy crucified feet;
By faith, for my cleansing, I see thy blood flow,—
Now was me, and I shall be whiter than snow.

4 The blessing by faith I receive from above;
O glory! my soul is made perfect in love;
My prayer has prevailed, and this moment I know
The blood is applied,—I am whiter than snow.

41

COME, sinners, to the gospel feast;
It is for you, it is for me ;
Let ev'ry soul be Jesus' guest :
It is for you, it is for me.

CHO.—Salvation full, salvation free,
The price was paid on Calvary ;
O weary wand'rer, come and see,
It is for you, it is for me.

2 Ye need not one be left behind,
For God hath bidden all mankind,

3 Sent by my Lord, on you I call ;
The invitation is to all :

4 Come, all the world ! come, sinner, thou !
All things in Christ are ready now.

5 Come, all ye souls by sin oppressed,
Ye restless wanderers after rest ;

6 Ye poor, and maimed, and halt, and blind
In Christ a hearty welcome find.

42

Music No. 378 in " The Quartet."

GO and tell Jesus, O desolate heart,
Go and tell Jesus how weary thou art;
Weary of trying without him to live,
Seeking for comfort the world cannot give.

CHO.—Go and tell Jesus,—
Tell him how weary thou art,
Go, thy Saviour is waiting,
Waiting to comfort thy heart.

2 Go and tell Jesus, so ready to hear,
Whisper thy sorrow alone in his ear;
Long hast thou grieved him, but still he is kind;
Ask, he will give thee; go, seek thou and find.

3 Narrow the gate, but a light thou wilt see
Shining above it, and shining for thee;
Go, and, believing, acknowledge thy sin;
Knock, he will open and welcome thee in.

4 Go and tell Jesus thy soul is oppressed,
Go and tell Jesus 'tis longing for rest,
Helpless, dependent, bend low at his throne,
Clinging by faith to his merits alone.

43

I WILL sing you a song of a beautiful land,
The far away home of the soul,
‖: Where no storms ever beat on the glittering strand,
While the years of eternity roll. :‖

2 Oh, that home of the soul in my visions and dreams,
Its bright, jasper walls I can see;
‖: Till I fancy but thinly the vail intervenes
Between the fair city and me. :‖

3 That unchangable home is for you and for me,
Where Jesus of Nazareth stands:
‖: The King of all kingdoms forever, is he,
And he holdeth our crowns in his hands.:‖

4 Oh, how sweet it will be in that beautiful land,
So free from all sorrow and pain;
‖: With songs on our lips and with harps in our hands
To meet one another again. :‖

29

HEAR the footsteps of Jesus,
  He is now passing by,
Bearing balm for the wounded,
  Healing all who apply;
As he spake to the suff'rer
  Who lay at the pool,
He is saying this moment,
  " Wilt thou be made whole?"

REF.—Wilt thou be made whole?:‖
  Oh, come, weary suff'rer,
    Oh, come, sin-sick soul ;
  See, the life-stream is flowing,
    See, the cleansing waves roll,
  Step into the current
    And thou shalt be whole.

2 'Tis the voice of that Saviour,
    Whose merciful call
  Freely offers salvation
    To one and to all;
  He is now beck'ning to him
    Each sin-tainted soul,
  And lovingly asking,
    " Wilt thou be made whole?"

3 Are you halting and struggling,
    O'erpowered by your sin?
  While the waters are troubled
    Can you not enter in?
  Lo, the Saviour stands waiting
    To strengthen your soul,
  He is earnestly pleading,
    " Wilt thou be made whole?"

4 Blessed Saviour, assist us
    To rest on thy word;
  Let the soul-healing power
    On us now be outpoured:
  Wash away every sin-spot,
    Take perfect control,
  Say to each trusting spirit,
    " Thy faith makes thee whole."

45

IN this world of burden bearing
   Help a little, help a little;
For thy weary brother caring,
   Help just a little.

CHO.—Oh, the shoulders we might lighten!
   Oh, the paths that we might brighten!
   Oh, the wrongs that we might righten!
   Helping just a little.

2 In the work around us pressing
   Help a little, help a little;
 Let thy labor prove a blessing,
   Help just a little.

3 In the seed-time's early sowing
   Help a little, help a little;
 On the soil some care bestowing,
   Help just a little.

46   *Music No. 35 in " Radiant Songs."*

ALL for Jesus ! all for Jesus !
   All my being's ransomed powers :
All my thoughts, and words, and doings,
   All my days, and all my hours.

CHO.—All for Jesus ! blessed Jesus !
   All for Jesus gladly I resign !
   All for Jesus ! blessed Jesus !
   I am his and he is mine.

2 Let my hands perform his bidding,
   Let my feet run in his ways,—
 Let my eyes see Jesus only,
   Let my lips speak forth his praise.

3 Oh, what wonder ! how amazing !
   Jesus, glorious King of kings,—
 Deigns to call me his beloved,
   Lets me rest beneath his wings.

47

OH, blessed fellowship divine!
  Oh, joy supremely sweet!
Companionship with Jesus here
  Makes life with bliss replete;
In union with the purest one
I find my heaven on earth begun.

CHO.—Oh, wondrous bliss! oh, joy sublime!
  I've Jesus with me all the time. :‖

2 I'm walking close to Jesus' side,
    So close that I can hear
  The softest whispers of his love,
    In fellowship so dear,
  And feel his great, almighty hand
  Protects me in this hostile land.

3 I'm leaning on his loving breast,
    Along life's weary way;
  My path, illumined by his smiles,
    Grows brighter day by day;
  No foes, no woes my heart can fear
  With my almighty Friend so near.

4 I know his shelt'ring wings of love
    Are always o'er me spread,
  And though the storms may fiercely rage,
    All calm and free from dread,
  My peaceful spirit ever sings,
  "I'll trust the covert of thy wings."

48

HOW bright the hope that Calv'ry brings,
    Where love divine and mercy blends;
How full the joy that all may find,
  Where flows the blood can save and cleanse.

CHO.—I am glad there is cleansing in the blood, :‖
  Tell the world, all the world.
  There is cleansing in the Saviour's blood.

2 'Tis there! 'tis there the soul may go,
  And wash its sins and stains away;
Who gives up all,—who comes by faith,
  This cleansing finds without delay.

3 Speak, speak to Zion's burdened ones,
    Lead, lead them up to Calv'ry's Mount;
  The want of aching hearts is met,
    'Tis cleansing in redemption's fount.

4 Why need we struggle on in self,
    We cannot make one black spot white;
  'Tis Christ's own blood, and that alone,
    Can change and cleanse the heart aright.

5 I come! I come! and glad I am
    That Jesus calls the lost and vile;
  There thousands have a cleansing found,
    I'll heed the Saviour's welcome smile.

49   *Tune, "Sweet by and by."*

HOW tedious and tasteless the hours
    When Jesus no longer I see!
  Sweet prospects, sweet birds and sweet flowers
    Have all lost their sweetness to me;
  The midsummer sun shines but dim,
    The fields strive in vain to look gay;
  But when I am happy in him,
    December's as pleasant as May.

Cho.—   I believe Jesus saves,
    And his blood washes whiter than snow. :‖

2 His name yields the richest perfume,
    And sweeter than music his voice;
  His presence disperses my gloom,
    And makes all within me rejoice;
  I should, where he always thus nigh,
    Have nothing to wish or to fear;
  No mortal so happy as I,
    My summer would last all the year.

3 Content with beholding his face,
    My all to his pleasure resigned,
  No changes of season or place
    Would make any change in my mind:
  While blest with a sense of his love,
    A palace a toy would appear;
  And prisons would palaces prove,
    If Jesus would dwell with me there.

50

O FOR a heart to praise my God,
   A heart from sin set free!
A heart that always feels thy blood,
   So freely spilt for me!

2 A heart resigned, submissive, meek,
   My great Redeemer's throne;
Where only Christ is heard to speak,
   Where Jesus reigns alone.

3 O for a lowly, contrite heart,
   Believing, true, and clean,
Which neither life nor death can part
   From him that dwells within!

4 A heart in every thought renewed,
   And full of love divine;
Perfect, and right, and pure, and good,
   A copy, Lord, of thine.

5 Thy nature, gracious Lord, impart;
   Come quickly from above;
Write thy new name upon my heart,
   Thy new, best name of Love.

51

I WAS once far away from the Saviour,
   And as vile as a sinner could be,
‖:I wondered if Christ the Redeemer
   Could save a poor sinner like me.:‖

2 I wandered on in the darkness,
   Not a ray of light could I see,
‖:And the thought filled my heart with sadness,
   There's no hope for a sinner like me.:‖

3 And then, in that dark lonely hour,
   A voice sweetly whispered to me,
‖:Saying, Christ the Redeemer has power
   To save a poor sinner like me.:‖

4 I listened, and lo! 'twas the Saviour
   That was speaking so kindly to me:
‖:I cried, I'm the chief of sinners,
   Thou canst save a poor sinner like me.:‖

5 I then fully trusted in Jesus,
  And oh, what a joy came to me:
‖:My heart was filled with his praises,
  For saving a sinner like me. :‖

6 No longer in darkness I'm walking,
  For the light is now shining on me,
‖:And now unto others I'm telling,
  How he saved a poor sinner like me. :‖

7 And when life's journey is over,
  And I the dear Saviour shall see,
I'll praise him forever and ever,
  For saving a sinner like me.

52 *Temple Songs, No. 93.*

JESUS, my Saviour, to Bethlehem came,
  Born in a manger to sorrow and shame—
Oh, it was wonderful, blest be his name !
  ‖:Seeking for me, for me, :‖
  ‖:Seeking for me, seeking for me, :‖
Oh, it was wonderful, blest be his name !
  Seeking for me, for me.

2 Jesus, my Saviour, on Calvary's tree
Paid the great debt, and my soul he set free,
Oh, it was wonderful, how could it be?
  ‖:Dying for me, for me, :‖
Oh, it was wonderful, how could it be?
  Dying for me, for me.

3 Jesus, my Saviour, the same as of old,
While I did wander afar from the fold,
Gently and long he hath pled with my soul,
  ‖:Calling for me, for me, :‖
Gently and long he hath pled with my soul,
  Calling for me, for me.

4 Jesus, my Saviour, shall come from on high;
Sweet is the promise as weary years fly ;
O I shall see him descending the sky,
  ‖:Coming for me, for me, :‖
O I shall see him descending the sky,
  Coming for me, for me,

PLUNGED in a gulf of dark despair,
  We wretched sinners lay,
Without one cheering beam of hope,
  Or spark of glimmering day.

CHO.—The half has never yet been told,
  Of love so full, so free ;
The half has never yet been told,
  The blood it cleanseth me.

2 With pitying eyes the Prince of grace
  Beheld our helpless grief:
He saw, and, O amazing love!
  He ran to our relief.

3 Down from the shining seats above,
  With joyful haste he sped,
Entered the grave in mortal flesh,
  And dwelt among the dead.

4 O for this love let rocks and hills
  Their lasting silence break ;
And all harmonious human tongues,
  The Saviour's praises speak.

5 Angels, assist our mighty joys;
  Strike all your harps of gold ;
But when you raise your highest notes,
  His love can ne'er be told.

KEEP looking unto Jesus as we march along,
  Keep looking unto Jesus all the day,
When our hopes are steadfast and our hearts are strong,
  We can tread the narrow way.

CHO.—Keep looking unto Jesus, looking unto Jesus,
  Looking unto Jesus every day.
Till our cares grow lighter and our hopes grow
  And our sorrows flee away.   [brighter,

2 Keep looking unto Jesus with the night around,
  Keep looking unto Jesus, Star and Sun.
We shall yet behold him with full glory crowned,
  When the final vict'ry's won.

3 Keep looking unto Jesus when the storms are out,
  Keep looking unto Jesus, sorely tried;
We shall win the battle with a song and shout;
  We shall find new strength supplied.

4 Keep looking unto Jesus, Author of our faith,
  Keep looking unto Jesus as we move,
We shall share his triumph over sin and death,
  We shall reign with him above.

55 *Music No. 39 in "The Quartet."*

I HAVE laid my burden down where the crim-
    son waters flow,
  There's a blessing at the cross for me;
I have found a spring of joy that the world can
    never know,
  There's a blessing at the cross for me.

CHO.—Praise the Lord! praise the Lord! hallelujah!
    Still my happy, happy song shall be;
  I have found a spring of joy that the world can
    never know,
  There's a blessing at the cross for me.

2 I have laid my burden down, and my troubled
    heart is still,
  There's a blessing at the cross for me;
I am learning there by faith my Redeemer's gra-
    cious will,
  There's a blessing at the cross for me.

3 I have laid my burden down; oh, the peace that
    fills my soul!
  There's a blessing at the cross for me;
I was dead but now I live, since my Saviour made
    me whole,
  There's a blessing at the cross for me.

4 I have laid my burden down, and my Saviour gives
    me rest,
  There's a blessing at the cross for me!   [breast,
I can pillow now my head on his gentle, loving
  There's a blessing at the cross for me.

37

O HAPPY day that fixed my choice
   On thee, my Saviour and my God!
Well may this glowing heart rejoice,
   And tell its raptures all abroad.

2 O happy bond, that seals my vows
   To him who merits all my love!
Let cheerful anthems fill his house,
   While to that sacred shrine I move.

3 'Tis done, the great transaction's done;
   I am my Lord's and he is mine;
He drew me, and I followed on,
   Charmed to confess the voice divine.

4 Now rest, my long-divided heart;
   Fixed on this blissful center, rest;
Nor ever from thy Lord depart,
   With him of every good possessed.

5 High Heaven, that heard the solemn vow,
   That vow renewed shall daily hear,
Till in life's latest hour I bow,
   And bless in death a bond so dear.   P. DODDRIDGE

OH, this uttermost salvation!
   'Tis a fountain full and free,
Pure, exhaustless, ever flowing,
   Wondrous grace! it reaches me!

CHO.—It reaches me! it reaches me!
   Wondrous grace! it reaches me!
   Pure, exhaustless, ever flowing,
   Wondrous grace! it reaches me!

2 How amazing God's compassion,
   That so vile a worm should prove
This stupendous bliss of heaven,
   This unmeasured wealth of love!

3 Jesus, Saviour, I adore thee!
   Now thy love I will proclaim,
I will tell the blessed story
   I will magnify thy name!

58

DOWN at the cross where my Saviour died.
Down where for cleansing from sin I cried;
There to my heart was the blood applied;
    Glory to his name.

  Cho.—   Glory to his name ; :‖
    Now to my heart is the blood applied;
    Glory to his name,

2 I am so wondrously saved from sin,
Jesus so sweetly abides within ;
There at the cross where he took me in ;
    Glory to his name.

3 Oh, precious fountain, that saves from sin,
I am so glad I have entered in ;
There Jesus saves me and keeps me clean,
    Glory to his name.

4 Come to this fountain, so rich and sweet;
Cast thy poor soul at the Saviour's feet;
Plunge in to-day, and be made complete;
    Glory to his name.

59

I PRAISE the Lord that one like me
For mercy may to Jesus flee,
He says that whosoever will
May seek and find salvation still.

  Cho.—My Saviour's promise faileth never;
    He counts me in the Whosoever. :‖

2 I was to sin a wretched slave,
But Jesus died my soul to save ;
He says that whosoever will
May seek and find salvation still.

3 I look by faith and see this word,
Stamped with the blood of Christ **my Lord**
He says that whosoever will
May seek and find salvation still.

4 I now believe he saves my soul,
His precious blood hath made me whole;
He says that whosoever will
May seek and find salvation still.

60

I HAVE found a friend in Jesus, he's everything to
H 's the fairest of ten thousand to my soul; [me,
The Lily of the Valley, in him alone I see
All I need to cleanse and make me fully whole;
In sorrow he's my comfort, in trouble he's my stay,
He tells me every care on him to roll.
He's the Lily of the Valley, the bright and Morning
He's the fairest of ten thousand to my soul. [Star.

CHO.—In sorrow he's my comfort, in trouble he's my stay,
He tells me every care on him to roll.
He's the Lily of the Valley, the bright and Morning
He's the fairest of ten thousand to my soul. [Star.

2 He all my griefs has taken, and all my sorrows borne;
In temptation he's my strong and mighty tower;
I have all for him forsaken, and all my idols torn
From my heart, and now he keeps me by his power;
Though all the world forsake me, and Satan tempts me
Through Jesus I shall safely reach the goal. [sore,
He's the Lily of the Valley, the bright and Morning
He's the fairest of ten thousand to my soul. [Star.

3 He will never, never leave me, nor yet forsake me here,
While I live by faith and do his blessed will;
A wall of fire about me, I've nothing now to fear,
With his manna he my hungry soul shall fill;
Then sweeping up to glory to see his blessed face,
Where rivers of delight shall ever roll.
He's the Lily of the Valley, the bright and Morning
He's the fairest of ten thousand to my soul. [Star

61

SOFTLY and tenderly Jesus is calling,
Calling for you and for me,
See on the portals he's waiting and watching,
Watching for you and for me.

CHO.—Come home, come home,
Ye who are weary, come home,
Earnestly, tenderly Jesus is calling,
Calling, O sinner, come home!

2 Why should we tarry when Jesus is pleading,
    Pleading for you and for me?
Why should we linger and heed not his mercies,
    Mercies for you and for me?

3 Time is now fleeting, the moments are passing,
    Passing from you and from me;
Shadows are gathering, death-beds are coming,
    Coming for you and for me.

4 Oh, for the wonderful love he has promised,
    Promised for you and for me;   •
Though we have sinned he has mercy and pardon,
    Pardon for you and for me.

62   *Music No. 19 in "The Quartet."*

SHOULD the summons, quickly flying,
    On the slumb'ring nations fall,—
Lo! the heavenly Bridgroom cometh,
    Would the sound your souls appal?
    Are you ready? are you ready?
Should you hear the midnight call?

2 What if now the startling mandate
    Should the sleeping virgins hear,—
Are your lamps all trimmed and burning
    Should the Bridegroom now appear?
    Are you ready? are you ready?
Now to see your Lord appear?

3 Is there oil in all your vessels?
    Are your garments pure and white?
Are they washed in the cleansing fountain,
    Fit to stand in Jesus' sight?
    Are you ready? are you ready?
Are your lamps all clear and bright?

4 Rise! ye virgins,—sleep no longer,—
    Lest the call your souls surprise!
Lest ye fail to meet the Bridegroom,
    When he cometh from the skies.
    Oh, be ready! oh, be ready!
When he cometh from the skies;
    Oh, be ready! oh, be ready!
Hasten, from your slumbers rise!

THOUGH my sins where once like crimson red
To the healing stream my feet where led,
In the precious blood my Saviour shed
He washed me white as snow.

Cho.—O, my joyful song henceforth shall be,
'Tis the blood of Jesus cleanseth me,
Cleanseth, cleanseth,
Oh, yes, it cleanseth me.

2 •At the door of faith I entered in,
And to him confessed my guilt and sin,
With his own dear hand he washed me clean,
He washed me white as snow.

3 Though my heart was all I had to give,
Yet he smiled and bade me look and live,
What a calm, sweet peace did I receive,—
He washed me white as snow.

4 I will sing his power from death to save,
I will sing his triumph o'er the grave,
I will sing while crossing Jordan's wave,
He washed me white as snow.

TIDINGS, happy tidings, Hark! hark! the sound
Hear the joyful echo Thro' the world resound;
Christ the Lord proclaims them, Hear and heed the call
Come, ye starving ones that perish, Room, room for all

Ref.—Whosoever asketh, Jesus will receive;
Whosoever thirsteth, Jesus will relieve;
See the living waters, Flowing full and free;
Oh, the blessed whosoever! That means me.

2 Tidings, happy tidings, Hark! hark! they say,
Do not slight the warning, Come, oh, come to-day;
Christ, our loving Saviour, still repeats the call,
Come, ye weary, heavy-laden, Room, room for all.

3 Tidings, happy tidings, Hark! hark! again!
Rushing o'er the mountain, Sweeping 'er the plain;
Onward goes the message, 'Tis the Saviour's call,
Come, for everything is ready, Room, room for all.

65 *Music No. 37 in "The Quartet."*

SHOULD the death-angel knock at thy chamber
  In the still watch of to-night,
Say, will your spirit pass into torment,
  Or to the land of delight?

CHO.—Say, are you ready? oh, are you ready
    If the death-angel should call?
    Say, are you ready? oh, are you ready?
    Mercy stands waiting for all.

2 Many sad spirits now are departing
  Into the world of despair;
Every brief moment brings your doom nearer;
  Sinner, O sinner, beware!

3 Many redeemed ones now are ascending
  Into the mansions of light;
Jesus is pleading, patiently pleading;
  Oh, let him save you to-night.

66 *Temple Songs, No. 64.*

GOD be with you till we meet again,
  By his counsels guide, uphold you,
  With his sheep securely fold you,
God be with you till we meet again.

CHO.—Till we meet, till we meet,
    Till we meet at Jesus' feet;
    Till we meet, till we meet,
    God be with you till we meet again.

2 God be with you till we meet again,
  'Neath his wings securely hide you;
  Daily manna still provide you,
God be with you till we meet again.

3 God be with you till we meet again,
  When life's perils thick confound you;
  Put his arms unfailing round you,
God be with you till we meet again.

4 God be with you till we meet again,
  Keep love's banner floating e'er you;
  Smite death's threatening wave before you,
God be with you till we meet again.

43

67 *Music No. 175 in "The Temple Trio."*

ONE more day its twilight brings,
    One more day its shadow flings;
One sweet hour of grateful prayer,
Calling to rest from toil and care.

CHO.—One day nearer the land of song,
    One day nearer the white-robed throng;
    There at the gate they watch and wait
    For a meeting that shall last forever.

2 One more day of conflict passed.
    One more victory gained at last;
    One sweet hour in praise to spend,
    While at a throne of grace we bend.

3 One more day of reaping o'er,
    One more sheaf to crown our store;
    One sweet hour to bathe the soul
    Hear in the streams of joy that roll.

4 Saviour, when as now we rest,
    Leaning, trusting on thy breast,
    We shall cross the narrow sea
    Still may we sing, inspired by thee.

68 *Music No. 79 in "The Temple Trio."*

IS there any one here that is willing to-day
    On Jesus the Lord to believe?
Is there any poor soul that is longing to-day
    The gift of his grace to receive.

CHO.—Come unto me, come unto me;
    Jesus is calling, calling now to thee,
    Come, oh, come unto me.

2 Is there any one here that is trying to-day
    The fetters of evil to break?
Any ready to follow the Saviour to-day,
    And take up the cross for his sake.

3 Is there any one here that is weary to-day,
   Or laden, or sorrow oppressed?
   Is there any sad heart that is praying to-day
   To find in the Saviour a rest.

4 Hear the Saviour's sweet voice while he calls thee
   O come, and believe, and obey;   [again,
   He is waiting to bless, he will comfort thee now!
   He never turned any away.

69   *Music No. 68 in " The Quartet."*

AT the sounding of the trumpet, when the saints
   are gathered home,
We will greet each other by the crystal sea,
With the friends and all the loved ones there await-
   ing us to come,
What a gath'ring of the faithful that will be!

Cho.—   What a gath'ring, gath'ring,
       At the sounding of the glorious jubilee!
       What a gath'ring, gath'ring,
       What a gath'ring of the faithful that will be!

2 When the angel of the Lord proclaims that time
   shall be no more,
We shall gather, and the saved and ransomed see,
Then to meet again together, on the bright celestial
   shore,
What a gath'ring of the faithful that will be!

4 At the great and final judgment, when the hidden
   comes to light,
When the Lord in all his glory we shall see,
At the bidding of our Saviour, "Come, ye blessed, to
   my right,"
What a gath'ring of the faithful that will be!

4 When the golden harps are sounding, and the angel
   bands proclaim,
In triumphant strains, the glorious jubilee,
Then to meet and join to sing the song of Moses and
   the Lamb,
What a gath'ring of the faithful that will be!

70

ONLY a look, my Saviour,
  While trembling here I bow,
Only a look, my Saviour,
  My heart is breaking now.

CHO.—Only a look, only a look,
  Only a look from thee;
One look from the cross, the blood-stained cross,
  Will bring }
4th verse—Has brought } sweet peace to me.

2 Only a look, my Saviour,
  Will all my sins forgive,
Tenderly now behold me,
  And bid my Spirit live.

3 Only a look, my Saviour,
  With joy my heart would fill,
Graciously hear my pleading,
  And bend my wayward will.

4 Only a look, my Saviour,
  'Tis done, the work is thine,
Thou, by a look, hast made me
  An heir of grace divine.

71

I HAVE found a friend divine,
  Wont you love him too?
I am his and he is mine,
  Wont you love him too?

CHO.—Wont you love my Jesus,
  My precious, precious Jesus?
Wont you love my Jesus?
  He is waiting now for you.

2 Oh, how dear his name to me,
  Wont you love him too?
None can save your soul but he,
  Wont you love him too?

3 Heavy laden, care-oppressed,
  Wont you love him too?
How he longs to give you rest,
  Wont you love him too?

4 Cast your burden at his feet,
  Wont you love him too?
  There is pardon pure and sweet,
  Wont you love him too?

72   *Music No. 148 in "The Temple Trio."*

THERE'S a stranger at the door, let him in,
  He has been there oft before, let him in,
  Let him in ere he is gone,
  Let him in, the Holy One,
Jesus Christ, the Father's Son, let him in.

2 Open now to him your heart, let him in,
If you wait he will depart, let him in;
  Let him in, he is your Friend,
  He your soul will sure defend,
He will keep you to the end, let him in.

3 Hear you now his loving voice? let him in,
Now, oh, now make him your choice, let him in,
  He is standing at the door,
  Joy to you he will restore,
And his name you will adore, let him in.

4 Now admit the heavenly Guest, let him in,
He will make for you a feast, let him in,
  He will speak your sins forgiven,
  And when earth ties all are riven,
He will take you home to heaven, let him in.

73   *Music No. 46 in "Songs of Triumph."*

'TIS so sweet to trust in Jesus,
  Just to take him at his word;
Just to rest upon his promise;
  Just to know, "Thus saith the Lord."

REF.—Jesus, Jesus, how I trust him;
      How I've proved him o'er and o'er;
    Jesus, Jesus, precious Jesus!
      O for grace to trust him more.

2 O, how sweet to trust in Jesus,
  Just to trust his cleansing blood;
Just in simple faith to plunge me
  'Neath the healing, cleansing flood.

3 Yes 'tis sweet to trust in Jesus,
   Just from sin and self to cease;
Just from Jesus simply taking
   Life, and rest, and joy and peace.

4 I'm so glad I learned to trust thee,
   Precious Jesus, Saviour, Friend;
And I know that thou art with me,
   Wilt be with me to the end.

74

A BEAUTIFUL land by faith I see,
   A land of rest from sorrow free:
The home of the ransomed, bright and fair,
And beautiful angels, too, are there.

CHO.—Will you go? will you go?
   Go to that beautiful land with me?
   Will you go? will you go?
   Go to that beautiful land.

2 That land is called the City of Light;
It never has known the shades of night;
The glory of God, the light of day,
Hath driven the darkness far away.

3 In vision I see its streets of gold,
Its gates of pearl I, too, behold,
The river of life, the crystal sea,
The ambrosial fruit of life's fair tree.

4 The ransomed throng, arrayed in white,
In rapture range the plains of light;
In one harmonious choir they praise
Their glorious Saviour's matchless grace.

www.ingramcontent.com/pod-product-compliance
Lightning Source LLC
Chambersburg PA
CBHW030722110426
42739CB00030B/1349